THE KING'S SOCKS

RODERICK HUNT

Pictures by Valeria Petrone

Oxford University Press

1996

'It's my birthday quite soon,
hooray!' said the King.
'But this year, what presents
can everyone bring?'

‘I’ve got a new crown,
and I’ve got a gold ring.
I’ve plenty of silver,
and that sort of thing.’

The Queen gave a sigh,
as from a best jug
she poured some more tea
in her favourite mug.

Then she looked at the King
with a frown on her face,
'You must mend your socks,
they're such a disgrace.'

'Socks!' cried the King,
with a shout of delight.
'To think that I worried
and fretted all night.'

'That's a good present
to give to a king!
Call my Prime Minister!
Socks are the thing!'

The Minister came,
he was getting quite old.
And he did have a
terrible, terrible cold.

With his nose all bunged up,
and a pain in one ear,
with a cold in his head –
well, he just couldn't hear.

'Yes – socks for my birthday.
I'd like lots and lots.
I'd like some with stripes,
and I'd like some with spots.'

'I want thick woolly socks,
I want socks that are snug –
so my feet are as warm
as a bug in a rug!'

The Minister gave his
thin shoulders a shrug.
He sighed, and he gave his
white beard a sharp tug.

He was used to surprises,
and quite used to shocks.
But what would the King want
with dozens of *clocks*?

The King's birthday came.
What a terrible shock!
People came calling,
each one with a clock.

'If your majesty pleases,
we are happy to bring
these clocks, for a very fine,
jolly good King.'

There were dozens of clocks.
There were clocks big and small.
There were clocks for the kitchen,
the bedroom, the hall.

They binged and they chimed,
and they bonged and they whirred.
One sang like a cuckoo,
one chirped like a bird.

The King said, 'I can't sleep
for the bong and the bing,
and the tick and the tock,
and the chime and the ping.'

'And the dong and the ding,
and the tong and the ting,
and the clang of these clocks
all the time – how they ring!'

The King gave a groan,
'Oh these terrible clocks –
I'll hit them with hammers,
I'll smack them with rocks.'

'I'll smash them, I'll bash them,
I'll boil them and mash them,
I'll break them in pieces,
I'll bin them, I'll trash them!'

‘Oh stop!’ said the Queen,
‘You’re acting quite wild.
Just behave like a king,
and not like a child.’

'If it's driving you crazy,
the sound of these clocks,
well, let's ask the people
to swap them for socks.'

So wisely, the King did
just what the Queen said.
He swapped all the clocks,
and he got socks instead!